BOOK OF LEGAL STUFF

Other Books in This Series

BOOK OF BASEBALL STUFF

BOOK OF FOOTBALL STUFF

BOOK OF SUPERSTITIOUS STUFF

BOOK OF
Legal Stuff
And illegal!

Joanne O'Sullivan

Illustrated by Mike McCoy

imagine!
Publishing
New York
www.imaginebks.com

Text and art copyright © 2010 by Imagine Publishing, Inc.

Published by Imagine Publishing, Inc.
25 Whitman Road, Morganville, NJ 07751

Distributed in the United States of America by
BookMasters Distribution Services, Inc.
30 Amberwood Parkway, Ashland, OH 44805

Distributed in Canada by
BookMasters Distribution Services, Inc.
c/o Jacqueline Gross Associates, 165 Dufferin Street,
Toronto, Ontario, Canada M6K 3H6

Distributed in the United Kingdom by
Publishers Group UK
8 The Arena, Mollison Avenue, Enfield, EN3 7NL, UK

Library of Congress Cataloging-in-Publication Data

O'Sullivan, Joanne.
Book of legal stuff / Joanne O'Sullivan.
p. cm.
Includes index.
ISBN 978-1-936140-03-9
1. Law—Humor. I. Title.

K183.O88 2010
340—dc22
2009035042

Designed by Marc Cheshire
Printed in China

*This book is dedicated to those who make 'em
and those who break 'em.*

Contents

Opening Statements

Ladies and gentlemen of the jury, for your consideration: a collection of laws from around the world and around the block. These are the statutes, bylaws, ordinances, and amendments that govern our behavior and keep the world from devolving into sheer anarchy. These laws prevent us from eating pies baked by grandmothers in noncertified kitchens; make sure that we never accidentally get a glimpse of a sweaty naked person through a window; ensure that even in death, we will not be subjected to the poor taste of our loved ones who would carelessly put plastic flowers on our graves instead of real ones, thus endangering the lives and health of graveyard lawn maintenance technicians.

Be assured that somewhere, in a town hall, school board office, or Chinese provincial court of law, a group of your peers (or in some cases, a group of your great-grandparents'

Ladies and gentlemen of the jury, don't be fooled! These sweet-looking grandmothers are a menace to society.

peers) struggled to do justice. They sought to find the correct measures that would ensure that all of their constituents enjoyed equal protection and responsibility under the law, or at least that the people who complained the loudest would be satisfied and finally get out of their offices so they could go to lunch.

Ladies and gentlemen, feel free to laugh or even curse as you read (as long as you are not riding on a bus in Missouri, because then you might be ticketed for public indecency). But do not judge too harshly the people who made these laws. What would you do if faced with a team of high school basketball players who wantonly disregarded the state athletic association's regulations on stripes? How would you respond if people at your child's high school graduation just would not hold their applause until all the certificates had been handed out? I think that gives you an idea of the kinds of things that are at stake here.

If New Zealanders were allowed to have ferrets as pets or bars in Buenos Aries were allowed to raffle off boob jobs, what kind of world would it be? Not the kind of world you and I want to live in, I assure you. So ladies and gentlemen, as you read this book, rest assured that your best interests are being protected. You will be able to sleep better tonight knowing that there are no smelly people riding buses in your town (if you live in Bend, Oregon) and that no bongs are being sold in Israel. But if you live in Minnesota, please put your clothes on. It's illegal to sleep naked there.

Dissenting Opinions

MANY people are of the opinion that there are too many laws in this world. Do we really need rules to govern personal behavior on a bus or sidewalk? Do citizens really need to be told when to turn their stereos down? What to wear? Sometimes a law seems to go too far, but on the other hand, sometimes it's the public that's out of control. You be the judge: Are these laws sensible or simply silly?

AGGRAVATING CIRCUMSTANCES

In a perfect world, no one would mow a lawn at 6 A.M. on the weekend, and everyone would bathe before going to the library. Unfortunately, that's just not the world we live in. People have to be told to silence their excessively vocal cows and cars and not to rummage through other people's garbage. And if you think people are bad, wait till you read about the monkeys.

Bring on da Noise

In Lake Placid, New York, hooting is not allowed on the street after 9:30 P.M. Whistling, shouting, singing, and excessive horn honking is also banned. Hooters could face fifteen days of jail time.

In Bellows Falls, Vermont, a measure was proposed to lower the acceptable decibel of sound to 60, a level that would rule out most vacuum-cleaning activities.

It's illegal to mow your lawn on the weekend in Forte dei Marmi, Italy. In St. Petersburg, Florida, you have to wait until after 11 A.M. to do it.

A Scottish member of parliament called for a ban on high-heeled shoes worn in upper-floor flats. The noise made by the shoes on hardwood floors, he explained, was a nuisance to residents on the lower floors.

It's against the law to shoot a cannon close to a house in London. The infraction carries a fine of £200 (approximately $325). While you're in the city, you must also avoid wantonly discharging firearms, making bonfires, extinguishing gas lamps, or willfully disturbing residents by ringing their doorbells.

Musical Misdemeanors

The 1973 Christmas song "Merry Xmas Everybody" was banned from a London Holiday Inn's musical playlist after a "large proportion" of hotel guests reported the song too annoying.

In Scotland, players of the national instrument—the bagpipe—must play no louder than 85 decibels or else wear earplugs to ensure their health. Pipers say the typical level is 116 decibels and it's impossible to play with earplugs because the musicians can't hear to make adjustments to their own play-

*Jeeves couldn't understand why a little weekend
cannon firing would bother anyone.*

ing. Perhaps it's the rest of the population that should wear the earplugs!

Ice cream truck music is against the law in Stafford Township, New Jersey and Edmonston, Maryland. In Las Vegas, it can't be played after 7 P.M. Boston also considered a ban, and in Brooklyn, a group of citizens teamed up to fight the "annoying jingles" that no one can seem to get out of their heads. A Portsmouth, Virginia ice cream man sued to have his town's ban lifted.

In St. Petersburg, a woman sued her eighteen-year-old neighbor for "audio terrorism" because of her tendency to blast music from her car stereo that caused the neighbor's windows and doors to rattle and dogs to start barking.

Barking Mad

In Clifton, New Jersey, dogs are permitted to bark no more

than thirty minutes at a time.

In Riverside, California, owners must take action to restrain their excessive barkers within ten days of a reported violation. A repeat violation results in a fine of up to $500.

Deadly Weapons?

Two teen graffiti artists in England were banned from carrying felt-tipped pens and spray paint in public and banished from their hometown of Manchester until their eighteenth birthdays because of their repeated arrests for vandalism.

A man in Kent, England was also banned from owning felt-tip pens because of his propensity to graffiti on bathroom walls and buses.

In Madison, New Jersey, it's illegal to put a piece of fruit in a public place where someone might slip on it and fall.

Identity Theft

According to US federal law, it's illegal to impersonate Smokey the Bear or Woodsy the Owl.

In Rhode Island it's illegal to impersonate a fence viewer, an auctioneer, or corder of wood (whatever that is). In Missouri, it's illegal to pretend to be blind in order to secure something of value.

In the if-he-only-had-a-brain department: A New Hampshire man was barred from standing in his own field pretending to be a scarecrow and then becoming animated when people drove by. This behavior startled passersby so much that several near accidents happened on the road in front of his property.

Good Fences Make Good Neighbors

An eighty-eight-year-old Ohio woman was arrested after re-

If he only had a brain.

fusing to give back a football that her annoying Dennis-the-Menace-type thirteen-year-old neighbor had lobbed into her yard. The football was only the latest in a series of objects that he and the other neighborhood rascals had "carelessly tossed" into her yard, she said. She was charged with misdemeanor theft, but the charge was later dropped. The woman then sued the boy's parents for emotional distress.

Hit the Road, Granny

In Wales, an elderly woman became such a nuisance that she was banned from her hometown and ordered to go live in a nursing home in a nearby village. The eighty-two-year-old had embarked upon what neighbors called "an eight-year campaign of hate" and had already served six months in prison for a range of "anti-social behavior" including: harassing neighbors with verbal abuse, threatening to kill a neighbor's dog, attacking another with a walking cane, and mooning people.

Commencement Crimes

Seven people were arrested in South Carolina for failing to hold their applause until all the graduates had been announced at a high school graduation.

In Illinois, five students were denied their diplomas when their loving friends and families failed to hold their applause. The students had to do eight hours of public service before they could get their hands on their degrees.

Public Nuisances

In Brighton, Michigan, it's against the law to be annoying. More specifically, residents can't "repeatedly commit acts that alarm or seriously annoy another person and that serve no legitimate purpose" or "insult, accost, molest, or otherwise annoy, either by word of mouth, sign or motion any person in any public place." This is the sort of law that makes you think twice before taking your kids out anywhere!

In Newark, New Jersey it's against the law to stand on a street corner and make annoying remarks to passing pedestrians.

The public library system in Schaumburg, Illinois has banned people with "offensive bodily odors" from library use. That includes both odors associated with lack of bathing or those associated with excessive perfume.

In Natchez, Mississippi, dogs who rummage through garbage get off with a "mischievous animal" citation, while people who rummage through their neighbors' garbage get a trespassing ticket.

MATERIAL BREACHES

Crimes of fashion occur everywhere, everyday: white shoes after Labor Day, plaids and stripes together, Members Only jackets. . . . The punishment for these offenses is rarely worse than a raised eyebrow, a slight snicker, or an off-handed comment such as, "Nice jacket." But in some places, what you wear (or don't wear) is not just a matter of taste—it's the law.

From the Fashion Police Files

Until recently, it was illegal to wear pants with hip pockets in South Carolina. The well-positioned pouches could be used as a hiding place for a hip flask.

It's against the law to wear a hat (or a bonnet) in a movie theater in West Virginia.

It's illegal to wear a suit of armor in the British Houses of Parliament according to a law that's been on the books since 1279.

In Athens, Greece, it's against the law to wear stiletto heels while visiting the Acropolis. Meanwhile, the British amuse-

"Nice heels, Timmy."
"Thanks, where'd you get those shoes?"

ment park Alton Towers has banned children from wearing high heels that make shorter kids tall enough to meet the height requirement on rides.

In Yorkshire, England, it's against the law to wear a hat in a pub. The law is intended to help police better identify criminals on video surveillance footage.

Another Reason to Mope

In Russia, goth and emo styles are prohibited in schools and public buildings. The government says that the clothing and hairstyles express a negative attitude that leads to increased teen suicides.

Bikini Bans

Wearing a bikini off the beach is off limits in Capri, Italy; Dubai; and the island of Grenada.

Until recently, men on the beaches of Cape May, New Jersey were banned from wearing Speedos and going topless. A man on Bonita Beach, Florida was issued a ticket for wearing a Speedo. The judge dismissed the ticket, but the man sued.

Thong bathing suits are against the law in Myrtle Beach, South Carolina and Daytona and Ft. Lauderdale beaches in Florida.

In a related story, the state of New Jersey was considering a ban on bikini waxing, but reconsidered due to public outcry.

How Low Can You Go?

If you like to let your boxers show and your waistband ride low, low, low, you could be looking at some real trouble from the law. Towns all over the US, from Flint, Michigan and Hawkinsville, Georgia to Shreveport and Alexandria, Louisiana, have passed ordinances that make it illegal to wear pants with serious sag. A little boxer on display will get you a warning in Flint, but if the pants fall "below the buttocks" you could be looking at up to a $500 fine or up to a year in jail for disorderly conduct or indecent exposure. Lots of other towns and even states have proposed baggy pants bans, even some big cities, such as Atlanta, New Orleans, and the Chicago suburbs. But after a teenager in Riviera Beach, Florida was arrested and held in jail overnight for his droopy drawers in 2008, a local circuit judge ruled the town's ordinance unconstitutional. Free expression or fashion crime? The jury is still out.

Mini Skirting the Law

Mini skirts are forbidden at a Mexican university because the president said they "provoke attacks" on women. Meanwhile, a Ugandan minister proposed a mini skirt ban because they "distract drivers and lead to traffic accidents." During the 2008 Olympics in Beijing, women were banned from wearing mini skirts in the city. And finally, an Arizona woman was once banned from an airplane because of a too-short mini skirt.

No Nudes Is Good Nudes

The tiny canton of Appenzell, Switzerland has banned nude hiking. The offense had become so widespread that people from all over Europe had flocked to the area to hike in the buff. But opponents say the practice is not only immoral but also unsafe due to the dangerous exposure to UV rays at high altitudes. Now those hiking in the buff will face a 200 Swiss franc ($185) fine.

An Australian legislator introduced a ban on topless sunbathing, which is quite common at the country's beaches. In Romania, a measure was introduced to bar women over the age of sixty from going topless because they are "ugly" and might frighten away tourists. Law enforcement officials admitted that the sight of topless seniors often made them "sick."

Police in Poland have been cracking down on topless sunbathing on beaches, issuing tickets to women found violating the law. But the topless ban extends beyond real women to include mermaids. The official seal of the town of Ustka, which includes a bare-breasted mermaid, may no longer be publicly displayed by citizens and is now only visible on the town flag in the mayor's office.

A topless mermaid is also the symbol of the country's biggest city, Warsaw. But so far there has been no move to cover her up. On the other hand, topless bathing was recently legalized at pubic swimming pools in the city of Malmö in nearby Sweden.

In Villahermosa, Mexico, it's illegal to be nude even inside your home. The ban was set in place due to the proliferation of people in this very warm climate walking around in front of their windows au naturel. The penalty is over $100 for first time offenders or up to thirty-six hours of jail time.

A man in Scarborough, England, who enjoyed mowing his lawn in the buff, was banned by local lawmakers from going outside of his house outside of his clothes.

The laid-back town of Brattleboro, Vermont had to institute an emergency ban on public nudity after the town's teens got in the habit of hanging out in the central parking lot in the nude, doing things like holding hula hoop contests and riding bikes. When older people and even naturists from out of town started following suit, the town council decided it was time for action. After the emergency ban expired, the town council later voted to permit nudity again.

What Not to Wear While Driving

Innovative Nigerian motorcycle taxi drivers have tried to skirt the country's helmet law by strapping pumpkins, cooking pots, and rubber tires to their heads to keep the law, if not in letter, at least in spirit. The Road Safety Commission

Officer, can you tell us what time the hula-hoop contest is?

isn't really into the creative alternative thing: The drivers are fined and their motorcycles impounded.

Holy Cow!

A woman in Cincinnati was arrested for wearing a cow suit, chasing children, urinating on a porch and blocking traffic. The cow suit was only part of the larger charge of disorderly conduct.

Men in Skirts

The very same law that bans baggy pants landed a Clinton, Louisiana man in hot water. The man, who liked to wear a skirt while mowing his lawn, caught the attention of local officials who said his landscaping attire was an affront to public decency. Doctor's note in hand, the man explained that pants and shorts cause heat rash while he mows, while the skirt lets his skin breathe. The authorities were un-moved.

Apparently, underwear also caused chafing.

A Utah teen was sent home for wearing a kilt while he was doing a presentation on his Scottish heritage. The school principal did not recognize the kilt as an aspect of Scottish culture and accused the boy of cross-dressing.

PUBLIC DECENCY

Some people just cannot be trusted to uphold public decorum. It's a good thing there are laws to stop them from spitting their used chewing gum on the sidewalk and possibly even cursing while they're doing it. And then there are those intemperate individuals who would attempt to drink their firewater on the Lord's Day! You may be surprised to learn that some of these silly-sounding statutes aren't relics of a bygone era: They're brand new twenty-first-century laws.

Fussing Over Cussing

Public profanity is against the law in the British city of Preston and the US state of West Virginia. While most US states are striking antiquated profanity laws from the books, a legislator in South Carolina introduced a bill to enact one in that state in 2008.

Swearing and profane music are illegal in bars in St. Charles,

Missouri. The same statute also outlaws table dancing and drinking contests.

Singing profane or obscene songs or ballads or using any profane or obscene language is illegal in London according to a nineteenth-century law still on the books.

In 1999, a Michigan man capsized his canoe in the middle of the Rifle River and let loose a stream of expletives that could be heard loudly and clearly back on shore. A frightened mother with child in tow called the police on the potty-mouthed canoer and he was found guilty of violating a state code barring "indecent, immoral, obscene, vulgar, or insulting language in the presence or hearing of any woman or child." Three years and several appeals later, the charge was dropped.

It's against the law in Montreal, Canada to insult officers of the law by calling them pigs or donut eaters.

Spit Happens

In Calgary, Alberta, it's illegal to urinate, spit, or fight in public. It's also illegal to put your feet up on public benches. Saskatoon, Saskatchewan has a similar law that also includes public defecation (thank goodness!).

Spitting on the street is illegal in Guangzhou, Shanghai and Beijing, China. In Dubai, it can get you deported.

Spitting out your gum on the street is illegal in Prague, Czech Republic. In Singapore, you can't even chew it in public, let alone spit it out. You also can't feed birds or leave a public toilet unflushed in the sparkling clean and orderly country.

In Rhode Island, it's illegal to spit in any "equipment of public conveyance," in a public building, or on a sidewalk anywhere in the state. It's also illegal to spit in public in the town of Madison, New Jersey and the state of Louisiana. Doing so in Virginia could result in a $25 fine. In Palmyra, New York, spitting on the street can get you a $250 fine and up to fifteen days in jail.

Booze Bans

Beer and wine reviewers in Maryland are prohibited from receiving more than three samples of the product that they're reviewing.

It's against the law to be drunk in public in West Virginia, Georgia, California, Iowa, Pennsylvania, Indiana, and Kansas. Presumably you can be drunk in private.

Public drunkenness is also against the law in over 100 New Jersey towns, although it's legal in the state. In 36 states, you can be drunk in public as long as you're not also disorderly.

Waibter, wet me twy dhe wed again.

In Kentucky, bartenders can tell dead-beat dads to take a hike: It's illegal to sell alcohol to any man who has not "made proper provisions for his family."

In the UK, it's illegal to be drunk and in charge of a child under the age of seven.

Any food-serving establishment in Louisiana can get a liquor license except a donut shop.

Until very recently, it was illegal to sell alcohol at nudist colonies in California.

In Vermont you cannot have two glasses of beer in front of you at the same time.

It's illegal to buy alcohol on Election Day in Kentucky, Indiana, South Carolina, Utah, Alaska, Massachusetts, and West Virginia.

Students in the United States traveling abroad are held to the drinking age of their home states regardless of the drinking age in the country they are visiting.

South Carolina is really catching up with modern times. In 2008, the governor finally repealed the following law: "Once a year in October, all public schools should observe Frances Willard Day and "prepare and render a suitable program on the day to the end that the children of the state may be taught the evils of intemperance."

Boob Bans

In the Buenos Aires province in Argentina, authorities had to finally crack down on "boob-job raffles" after it became popular for local discos to raffle off opportunities for free breast enhancement surgery as a marketing stunt.

Book 'em!

Betting; gambling; using violent, abusive, or obscene language; or behaving in a disorderly manner in a library carries

Tipsy? In more ways than one.

a £200 ($325) fine in the UK under the 1898 Library Offences Act.

In Parsippany, New Jersey, hoarding library books is illegal and punishable by a $200 fine.

Wanna Bet?

In South Carolina, it's illegal to play card or dice games in your kitchen, barn, stable, or other "outhouses."

Online gambling is illegal in the US according to most state and federal laws. Once the law was passed, the operators of the online virtual world Second Life made online gambling illegal in their online world, but later repealed the law.

Those NCAA (National Collegiate Athletic Association) March Madness brackets you and your buddies fill out at work are actually illegal! Fantasy football is also technically illegal. A lawyer sued ESPN and CBS Sports for giving away prizes in their own fantasy football operations, but the suit was later thrown out. Betting on sports is illegal in all US states except Montana, Nevada, Oregon, and Delaware.

Protecting England's Queen Elizabeth, it appears, is not as demanding an occupation as you may think. Members of her royal protection guard were once arrested for running poker games during their downtime on the job. One officer said they could earn tens of thousands of pounds extra from this sideline "profession."

Kissdemeanors

Kissing and hugging in public are against the law in Kuala Lumpur, Malaysia. In India, it could get you a fine.

It's illegal to kiss on French trains, but there's no penalty for doing so. A similar ban at a train station in England was met by such an outcry that the station lifted the ban and the stationmasters established a designated kissing zone instead.

The mayor of Guanajuato, Mexico faced such a backlash over a proposed public kissing ban that he reversed course and invited all visitors to kiss with impunity in the "kissing capital of Mexico." The city of Moscow is considering a city-wide public kissing ban.

In Dubai, it's illegal to kiss or hold hands in public. Infractions may result in a prison sentence.

Teen kissing (under the age of sixteen) is against the law in South Africa.

"Displays of affection not appropriate in a public setting" are off-limits in several NFL (National Football League) stadiums, including Seattle, St. Louis, and Philadelphia.

Thou Shalt Not Shop

In West Virginia, it's illegal to sell a number of items on a Sunday, including footwear, athletic equipment, outdoor furniture, and semiprecious stones.

In Pennsylvania, you can sell stuff on Sunday as long as you have a note explaining that you don't observe Sunday as the Sabbath and as long as you don't disturb others who are observing the Sabbath.

The Bedroom Police

They say no one knows what goes on behind closed doors, but if anyone should find out, a bunch of folks could be in trouble. Fornication (sex between unmarried people) is still illegal in Massachusetts and punishable by up to three months in jail. However, if you'd like to have single sex, it's now legal to do so in Virginia, as long as you don't do anything nontraditional such as oral and anal sex, which is still illegal. Better stick to the missionary style in Maryland, too, or you could end up in jail for ten years!

Vibrators are against the law in Alabama.

Bigamy (multiple marriages) is considered a felony in Utah, but there are over 30,000 people living in polygamist families in the state.

Cheaters never prosper, and in Massachusetts, they could end up in jail for three years for breaking their marriage vows.

In Texas, public lewdness is against the law, but it's also against the law in private if someone who might be offended could be present.

In West Virginia, it's illegal to falsely accuse a woman of being unchaste.

According to a Russian news agency, two Russian tourists on vacation in Florida decided to challenge a wacky law they heard about: no sex with porcupines. The two gentlemen were later treated at a nearby hospital.

Cohabitation (that's "living together before you're married" for you young folks) is considered "lewd and lascivious" behavior and is illegal in Florida, North Dakota, Michigan, Mississippi, Virginia, and West Virginia. The punishments range from a $500 fine to a short prison sentence.

Four Out of Five Dentists Recommend Shivs

Standard toothbrushes (handle, brush on the tip) have been banned in Lee County, Florida correctional institutions because the prisoners alter them in attempts to use them as weapons, officials say. Instead, prisoners get specially designed toothbrushes with a circular opening that wraps around the finger (kind of like brass knuckles). While the move was not sparked by any incident, prison officials say that in cell searches, they frequently found toothbrushes that prisoners attempted to alter in some way, presumably not in order to improve their dental hygiene.

Dirty Dancing

In Iowa's largest city, Des Moines, it's illegal to dance in public between the hours 2 A.M. and 6 A.M., Monday through Saturday. Although lawmakers can't exactly trace the origin or purpose of the law, they know it's been on the books since 1942. Bars or clubs wishing to allow their patrons to dance during legal hours are required to pay a $200 annual fee for a license or $75 if it's just a onetime event. Officials are considering repealing the law, but say that there doesn't seem to be much public interest in dancing during those hours, anyway. Some tourism industry representatives are pushing for the change, though, in an effort to promote Des Moines as a more cosmopolitan "24-hour city."

YOUTHFUL OFFENDERS

Among the random and senseless laws of the world, a dispro-
portionately high number of them center on kids. Everyone
wants to protect children, even if it's only from themselves.
More often than not, these laws are meant to protect kids
from the lawsuit-happy parents of other kids.

Dangerous Games?

It's illegal to fly a kite in Chicago; Newark, New Jersey; and
London. It's not, however, illegal to shoot a gun in these
cities.

In London, it's also against the law to "use a slide upon ice or
snow" according to an 1872 statute that's still on the books.

A school in Queensland, Australia banned cartwheels and
other "unsupervised gym activities" on school playgrounds
in an effort to prevent injuries. The offense was punishable

*Jeffrey the gun-toting nine-year old only drew
his weapon against wrongdoers.*

with a potential suspension. The local education board later urged the school to repeal the ban.

Schools in Cheyenne, Wyoming and Attleboro, Massachusetts have outlawed the game of tag during recess as a measure to prevent parental lawsuits. A school in Charleston, South Carolina has banned all unsupervised contact sports after lunch for the same reason.

A school in Peterborough, England banned snowball fights on the playground. In North Wales, the snowball ban extends to all areas of the region.

In Lodi, California and Huntington, New York, it's illegal to use Silly String at parades.

Pokémon cards are prohibited in Kansas schools because of their content, which seems to support the concept of evolution.

Skateboarding Is NOT a Crime. Or Is It?

Skateboarding in an empty pool is illegal in California, but

Dude, I said EMPTY swimming pools.

after the foreclosure crisis left thousands of backyard pools empty in that state, clandestine pool skating skyrocketed. Creative skaters started using online realty search engines or Google Earth to locate foreclosed homes with empty pools.

For the Good of the Child

In Queensland, Australia, plastic surgery for cosmetic purposes is against the law for those under the age of eighteen.

Also in Queensland: Children who play in a local netball league are banned from eating oranges during halftime. Officials say the acidity in the fruit is dangerous to children's teeth when they are dehydrated.

In the let's-all-move-to-Canada department: An elementary school in Ontario banned homework. They cite the lack of evidence that it improves academic achievement. Perhaps that's the fault of Canadian researchers not doing *their* homework!

In Texas, truant students are required to wear GPS tracking anklets.

In Japan, teens are prohibited from taking Tamiflu, a flu treatment drug. The legal drug is common during flu season in many countries, but Japan banned it for teens after two boys jumped from the roofs of their houses and broke their legs after taking it. The company that manufactures Tamiflu says that the drug actually decreases adverse psychiatric responses in those who take it.

At Watercliffe Meadow Academy in Sheffield, England, the word "school" has been banned from school reports and replaced with "place for learning" in order to foster a more positive environment.

In France, television shows aimed at babies have been outlawed. The US is considering a similar ban.

In Florida, it's against the law for children to work in snake pits or in the field of alligator wrestling.

In Hanford, California, adults may not prevent children from jumping in puddles.

Cut Your Hair ... But Not Like That

A six-year-old in Ohio was suspended from school for coming in with a Mohawk haircut. School officials said the haircut was a distraction for other students and was disrupting the educational environment.

An eleven-year-old in Michigan was barred from school because her hair was dyed pink. The officials told her to come back to school when her hair was "normal" again.

Dress Code

In the Gonzalez, Texas school system, dress code violators

are required to wear a prison-style jumpsuit.

After an alarming number of students came to school with orange skin, a British school banned fake tans. No word on how they would ascertain the authenticity of a kid's "healthy glow."

A school district in Merrillville, Indiana banned students from wearing the color pink. The color was said to be associated with a local gang.

Killjoys at Work

The mayor of Eraclea, Italy banned building beach sandcastles.

A school in Litchfield, Connecticut banned any reference to Valentine's Day in the school's lesson plans and outlawed any celebrations of the day.

*My mom says I'm gonna get virtual cavities
from too much of this stuff.*

In Columbus, Nebraska, outdoor trick-or-treating is prohibited for kids of any age. In order to compensate, the town offered kids the opportunity to download pictures of candy from the Web sites of local businesses.

Throwing candy or beads from floats is prohibited in Plant City, Florida.

In Norfolk, England, children are not permitted to purchase ketchup or eggs from local supermarkets. Police enacted the ban after repeated incidents of attacks on homes and vehicles with the two aforementioned items. Police reported a dramatic decrease in the number of incidents since supermarket staff began to enforce the ban.

What's That Smell?
A middle school in Maine banned intentional flatulence. Apparently a group of eighth-grade boys had turned the production of naturally occurring gases into something of a game, which got out of control. The penalty for the infraction is detention.

In a related incident, a disruptive thirteen-year-old in Marin

County, California was arrested for continually passing gas and turning off other students' computers.

Cruel and Unusual Naming Practices

Election officials in the Dominican Republic recently decided enough was enough with the unique baby name craze that had taken over their country. One too many voters with names such as Toshiba, Mazda, and Winston Churchill tipped them off that things were getting out of hand. The arrival of Querida Pina (Dear Pineapple) was one of the last straws that sent the issue of legal names to a judge. The officials introduced legislation to ban exceptionally unusual baby names, but it didn't pass.

In Sweden, the tax authorities objected to a couple naming their baby Metallica, while a couple in the US had all their children taken away after an investigation that was sparked by a bakery that refused to print their youngest child's name—Adolph Hitler—on a birthday cake.

In New Zealand, a judge ruled that a couple couldn't name their child 4Real (because names can't start with a number), so they decided to name him Superman instead.

Little baby Krisis Mondial (World Crisis)—who arrived in Monterrey, Mexico just in time for the economic downturn of 2008—may face teasing at school, but her parents faced no restrictions in giving her such an unusual name.

Mosquito Swatters

Some clever techie came up with a gadget known as a mosquito tone—a ringtone so high-pitched that human adults can't hear it (although it may be heard by adult dogs AND children). The tone was designed to let kids get away with the mischievous crime of texting during class—if the teacher can't hear the tone, he or she can't confiscate the phone. The technology was then co-opted by mean adult storeowners who used it in a gadget called Teen Repellent, which emits a high-pitched sound. The sound annoys teens (but not adults!) and causes them to move on if they are thinking about loitering outside stores and not buying anything. The British city of Kent banned Teen Repellents in all its buildings because the technology unfairly targets youngsters.

Kids Will Be Kids

An eight-year-old in California stole his teacher's car and drove himself home from school. He was suspended.

Rules of
Order

IT's essential that business, traffic, government, and even sports proceed in an orderly fashion, and there are many useful laws to ensure that's what happens. It's easy to imagine the mayhem that would ensue if postal workers did their rounds with pet treats in their pockets or children set up lemonade stands willy-nilly, resulting in unfair competition for legitimate lemonade vendors. If a society is judged by the rules it creates, what do these ones say?

MOTIONS TO PROCEED

Everyone has to get from point A to point B. But how to get there is another question. On a bus? Make sure you don't let loose with an F-bomb if you're in Missouri. In a car? Don't shave while you're driving! Also, don't breastfeed while talking on your cell phone as you negotiate your vehicle. And please, don't ride your horse drunk, no matter where in the world you may live.

Rules of the Road

In Kuwait, it's illegal to drive a car that's more than ten years old.

It's illegal to run out of gas on the German autobahn. The penalty is approximately $100.

Street racing is illegal on public streets across the US, but there is a legal organization known as the Illegal Street Racing Organization.

It's illegal to drive a dirty car in Moscow.

A bill to ban black cars in California was introduced in 2009.

The City of Birmingham, England outlawed apostrophes on road and street signs.

In Aurora, Illinois, it's illegal to wave a flag out a car window.

In Florida, stunt riding (such as popping a wheelie) on your motorcycle could get you a ten-year ban on your motorcycle license or even jail time.

In Indiana, you can't get vanity plates with a reference to a deity on them. In Colorado, a tofu-lover's vanity plate was denied because officials considered it to be obscene: ILOVETOFU. (Think about it.)

In Arizona, the "stupid motorist law" states that anyone who drives around road barricades into a flood-prone portion of a road during a flash flood warning can be charged for his or her own rescue.

A driver in Denver was ticketed for driving in the HOV

Sorry, we don't take American Express.

(high occupancy vehicle) lane with a mannequin in the passenger seat. The driver said he was just giving her a lift. The dummy smartly remained silent.

Don't Cuss on the Bus

In Bend, Oregon, extremely smelly people can be prohibited from boarding a public bus. Those who pass the sniff test will not be allowed to spit once on the bus.

A disabled Ottawa woman was barred from entering a public bus with her "guide ferret" because the animal was causing distress to other riders and their service animals. The woman protested the ban, and the transportation company in charge of the bus later said it would allow the woman and her ferret back on the bus after an assessment by an animal behavior therapist determined that it was one of the best-behaved ferrets she had ever seen.

It's illegal to be drunk on a bus in Missouri unless it's a charter bus. It's also illegal to cuss on the bus, spit, or fail to obey a reasonable request from a bus driver. Cussing on the bus is also illegal in Utah.

In Henry County, Georgia an obese man was barred from riding local buses because the bus drivers could not handle the strain of lifting him and his wheelchair onto the bus.

In El Paso, Texas, it's against the law for an able-bodied person under the age of sixty-five to deny a seat to an elderly or disabled person.

Honk If You Love Free Expression

In Florida, "obscene" bumper stickers are outlawed, but there's no legal definition of obscenity.

The University of Illinois banned "partisan" bumper stickers on the cars of faculty and staff but later reversed the decision.

A Michigan law, which came to be known as the "fuzzy dice law," prohibits dangling air fresheners, Mardi Gras beads, fuzzy dice, or any other item that's large enough to obstruct a driver's view.

Truck Nutz, the "truck ornament" that resembles bull genitalia, are against the law in Florida, and Virginia and Maryland are considering a ban. The decorative truck accessory, which is typically hung from a truck's trailer hitch, was found by the state legislature to be excessively vulgar. The bill outlawing them also included a ban on dangling ornamental female breasts, human buttocks, or other animal genitalia.

A lawmaker in Arizona introduced a bill to ban naked lady mud flaps, but it was defeated.

The Huck Finn Statutes?

In Kentucky, it's illegal to beach or anchor your shanty boat on the land of another for more than twelve hours, except in the case of distress. Presumably if you are piloting a shanty boat in this day and age, you're already in some state of distress.

Drunken steam engine driving is prohibited in the UK.

Don't act suspicious around a steamboat landing or electric car rail depot in Massachusetts. You may be ticketed.

A group of Greenpeace activists was arrested for boarding a ship in Miami. Their crime? Boarding a vessel before it docks is prohibited according to an 1872 law against "sailor-mongering," the practice of kidnapping sailors from ships and getting them drunk in town so that possessions may be stolen from their ships while they are unaware.

With All Due Haste

In the UK, it's illegal to ride a horse "furiously" down the street.

A wheelchair-bound Scottish man was banned from renting wheelchairs at a local provider because he was caught on tape exceeding the speed limit for the chairs.

An English driver in a 1923 Model T was ticketed for going 55 in a 50-mph zone. Protesting the ticket, he claimed the car could only go 48 mph. His protest was denied because the car had no speedometer and therefore he could not prove its speed.

A driver in Montreal was charged with obstructing a police operation when he flashed his lights to warn other drivers of a speed trap ahead. The charge was later dismissed.

Keep Your Eyes on the Road

In Texas, you can be fined for multitasking on the go. Shaving, putting on makeup, or eating behind the wheel is off limits. Reading, writing, interacting with a pet or passenger,

Multi-tasking on the multi-lane led to a multi-car pileup.

using a fax machine or CD player, and of course, texting or talking on the phone while driving, could also get you in hot water. No word on whether or not picking your nose is allowed.

In England, a health and safety expert was banned from driving for six months when he was caught shaving in his car while driving 70 mph.

An Ohio woman was ticketed for breastfeeding an infant while driving. She was also talking on a cell phone at the same time. Talk about a multitasking mom!

No Honk Day

In Mumbai—one of the noisiest cities in the world—officials designated World Health Day as a "no honking" day in order to raise awareness about the health effects of noise pollution.

There are an estimated 1.5 million motor vehicles in the city. On the no-honk day, more than 3,000 drivers were ticketed for violating the rule between the hours of 10 A.M. and 2 P.M. The fine for "excessive honking" was set at around $2.50.

Crossing the Line?

It's against the law to cross the street wearing headphones in New York City or Buffalo, New York. The same law bans talking on the phone or using a Blackberry.

While helping elderly passengers cross the street in a snowstorm, a Denver bus driver was hit by a pickup truck and suffered internal bleeding and broken bones. After his release from the hospital, he was ticketed for jaywalking.

RWI: Riding While Intoxicated

Under the state's public intoxication laws, a man in Cody, Wyoming was arrested for drunk driving in the middle of a snowstorm. He was riding a horse.

On the other hand, two drunken riders in Pennsylvania who were involved in an accident were not cited because their horses could not be classified as vehicles.

A man in Gloucester, England was ticketed for drunk riding a horse and carriage. He was in violation of an 1872 ordinance, which also includes the aforementioned drunken steam engine driving.

A man in Arvada, Colorado was fined $25 for drunken "joy riding" his horse through town.

Hands Off the Hard Body

In Clinton, Oklahoma, it's illegal to molest a vehicle.

A "car criminal" in York, England was banned from touching any car. The man, who had seventy-five car vandalism convictions, was also sentenced to four months in prison. His fingerprint was later found on a stolen car, landing him back in jail facing stiffer charges.

Getting Tough on Bike Crimes

It's illegal to ride a bike in a swimming pool in Baldwin Park, California.

An eight-year-old Florida boy was ticketed for failing to yield the right of way when he rode his bike over a dirt mound, onto the street, and into a car.

In Natchez, Mississippi, all bikes must be equipped with a bell or horn to ride on the city streets.

In New York, it's against the law to abuse airline passengers by leaving them sitting on the tarmac for an excessive amount

Hey fellas, wait for me!

of time without food, water, or access to bathrooms.

Only in freewheelin', beer-loving Holland can you find the beer bike: a ten-person, pedal-powered, mobile karaoke bar that riders can cruise around town in while enjoying a frosty mug and a song. Riders sit at a table under a canopy and enjoy beer while a designated driver pedals them through the city streets. But after a rash of accidents involving drunken riders falling off the vehicle, the Amsterdam city council is considering a measure that would restrict the bikes to pedestrian-only areas. The bike has already been banned in the city's famous red-light district.

LEGAL TRANSACTIONS

In the competitive world of commerce, sometimes it seems like anything goes. Well, not exactly. There are loads of laws that limit what you buy, who you can buy it from, how you buy it, where it is bought, and when you can buy it. (It's a wonder you can get a loaf of bread with all these laws on the books!) Laws are made to protect the consumer, the seller, and just to maintain some level of sanity in the world. However much you would like to, for example, you cannot sell your soul on eBay.

Not For Sale

Bottled water can't be sold at city facilities in Seattle, San Francisco, and London, Ontario. It's also unlawful to sell it at Ontario schools.

It's illegal to sell spray paint to minors in New Haven, Connecticut and Sparks, Nevada.

In Los Angeles, it's illegal to sell any item with a gang logo on it.

In Saudi Arabia, it's illegal to sell red roses and other red gift items in February. The law is designed to discourage people from trying to celebrate the Western holiday of Valentine's Day.

In Billings, Montana it's illegal to sell or give away rats except as food for snakes or birds of prey.

It's illegal to sell cat and dog fur in the European Union (unless it's still attached to the living animal.

EBay prohibited an English man who wanted to sell his entire life on the auction site because the item violated the company's policy. You also can't sell live animals, weapons of mass destruction, medical devices such as pacemakers, or the teacher's edition of textbooks (at least on the US eBay site).

Retail Realities
In Tennessee, retail stores can only be located on the first floor of a building and must have only one public entrance,

unless the store is a corner store, in which case, a door may be located on each of the streets it sits on.

A London man was arrested for poaching Wi-Fi from a business. Two men in Northumbria, England were arrested for using a neighbor's Wi-Fi without permission. A Michigan man was arrested for sitting in a parking lot outside a café to use its Wi-Fi to check his email on a daily basis.

An Arizona restaurant was fined for allowing its patrons to dance. According to the law governing restaurants, patrons can legally sway but not move their feet to the music.

The Queen Elizabeth Hotel in Montreal is required to provide food for your horse if you're a hotel guest.

Lemonade Crimes

Technically, it's illegal to sell lemonade at a stand in front

I'm afraid this establishment isn't up to code.

of your home. But who would shut down a young, up-and-coming entrepreneur? In Massachusetts, a competitive street sausage vendor shut down a pair of nine-year-olds who were infringing on his business.

In Florida, a complaining neighbor had a six-year-old shut down for selling lemonade without a license.

Second-Hand Blues

The trafficking in used schoolgirl panties, gym suits, school uniforms, and bathing suits at Tokyo sex shops got so out of hand that the city had to outlaw the practice.

Flea markets are against the law in Hialeah, Florida.

Used car lots are prohibited in downtown Binghamton, New York.

Legal Tender

In Canada, it's illegal to pay for a purchase over 25 cents in pennies. In the UK, merchants don't have to accept payment in pennies for goods over 20 pounds according to the 1971 Coinage Act.

Apparently paying in pennies is a universal way of showing displeasure with having to pay a parking or traffic ticket. An English court refused to accept the £400 ($660) fine payment made in pennies by a "careless driver" because of the aforementioned act. A man in New Jersey was arrested for trying to pay his traffic ticket in pennies, too. In the US, the practice is not illegal, but it's considered a nuisance.

Up in Smoke

It's illegal to sell single cigars in Prince George County, Maryland. The measure was designed to keep young people from purchasing one cigar, removing all the tobacco, and replacing it with marijuana.

It's illegal to sell bongs in Israel. In Philadelphia, they can't be sold within 500 feet of schools, churches, or community centers.

India passed its first law to ban kids from purchasing cigarettes in 2008.

Contraband

A librarian in Pennsylvania was arrested for selling discarded *National Geographic* magazines on eBay to raise money to buy computers for the library. The charge was theft of entrusted property. In another library crime, a man in Colorado was arrested for checking out books from the library and then selling them on eBay.

In Vedic, Iowa, non-organic food can't be sold within city

limits, although people can bring non-organic food into the city. The city was founded by Maharishi Mahesh Yogi (the founder and leader of the Transcendental Meditation movement) in the 1960s.

Notorious Possessions

Freshmen at one Chinese university are prohibited from owning computers as a measure to prevent them from becoming Internet addicts.

An English counterfeiter was barred from owning a photocopier, high-quality paper, or metal foil.

A Singapore man was banned from owning a camera phone after he was caught taking pictures under restroom stall doors.

Convicted drug dealers in Wales are prohibited from owning

more than one mobile phone.

Bad Ads

In France, it's against the law to promote extreme thinness by glamorizing it in advertising or using emaciated-looking models. It's also illegal to aim cell phone advertising at children in the country.

In the UK and Quebec, it's against the law to advertise junk food to kids. Several countries have considered banning all advertising aimed at children and it's already against the law in Sweden. Sweden has also moved to ban advertising that can be considered sexist.

In Madrid, Spain, businesses can no longer advertise via the "human billboard," otherwise known as the sandwich board person. The local government called the practice "an assault to human dignity." In the West End of London, it was outlawed because it causes too much clutter. In Redmond, Washington, any kind of human advertising is banned. That includes dancing pancakes, chickens, and gorillas.

Taxing Circumstances

In one Indian state, it's illegal to sell vibrating condoms. Officials say the product combines two things—a contraceptive and a pleasure enhancer—and therefore must comply with more stringent sex toy laws rather than looser contraceptive laws.

You can be taxed on the sale of illegal drugs in thirty US states. A Tennessee man who was selling pot-laced Rice Krispie treats at a concert received a tax bill for $11,506. He argued that the tax should only have been for the weight of the marijuana, not for the marshmallow and cereal in the treats.

In Nevada, a 10% sales tax is levied on nude or partially nude services such as food or beverages served by nude or scantily clad individuals. A New York legislator proposed a "lap dance tax." In England, those who perform lap dances or pole dances are responsible for paying the VAT (value-added tax) on the service.

In Alabama, playing cards are taxed an additional 10 cents on top of the regular sales tax.

In Chicago, fountain drinks are taxed at a rate of 9% while drinks sold in a can or bottle are taxed at 3%.

In several US cities and states, professional athletes of visiting teams are taxed for the portion of their income received while playing an away game in the state.

In Pennsylvania, West Virginia, Illinois, and Oklahoma,

those who bet at casinos pay taxes even if they don't win. There's a "wagering" tax in place.

Maine has a blueberry tax: Sellers of blueberries must pay the state 1.5 cents per pound of blueberries sold.

In Maryland, there's a "flush tax" on homes using municipal sewage. The tax was instituted to pay for a new sewage treatment plant.

What's in a Name?

In Pennsylvania, companies are prohibited from using blasphemous names, such as "I Choose Hell Productions" or "The God Damn Gun Shop."

In the EU (European Union), the makers of sunscreen cannot label their product as "sunblock" because no product completely "blocks" the sun. The product package cannot claim

Talk about throwing your money down the toilet!

"100% protection" for the same reason. Lawmakers say the rule is meant to decrease the high rate of skin cancer in the region and dispel the myth that wearing sunscreen is insurance against it. Along with the labeling requirements for sunscreen, officials have been under mounting pressure to ban tanning beds in the EU in the effort to prevent skin cancer.

LEGALLY EMPLOYED

Regulating the world of work requires a web of laws so thick you could skate across it (if that was legal). There are laws about who you can hire and fire, why and how, and then of course there are the laws that regulate what goes on in the office. Some companies monitor what you wear, but there are others that won't even let you complain about your job.

Company Policy

In Portugal, employees can't be fired. Ending an employment relationship is a complicated procedure, which can take several months.

The Supreme Court of India ruled that an employee cannot be sacked after he or she has already retired.

In Peru, you can't be fired for being drunk at work.

A Filipino immigrant in Australia was sacked for using "un-Australian" toilet habits.

In Murfreesboro, Tennessee, employees can be asked to leave work due to excessive body odor or excessive cologne or aftershave.

A city worker in Detroit sued to have perfumes banned from the workplace after experiencing an allergic reaction to a coworker's perfume.

In Australia and New Zealand, postal workers can be demoted for being overweight.

In Minneapolis, postal workers are prohibited from carrying dog treats.

A Chinese company banned its employees from bathroom breaks while at work. Those who use the bathroom can be fined 63 cents per visit.

A British bicycle company prohibits its employees from riding their bikes on official company business.

Technicalities

Facebook and other social networking sites are a minefield for employees. A recent survey said that over 60% of companies ban employees from using social networking sites while at work. Employees can be fired for tweeting on Twitter at work, blogging, or visiting sites with the word "blog" in them. In the case of one British teen, commenting that work is boring on your Facebook status led to dismissal. A California court ruled that an employee can't be fired for web surfing at work. And an Edinburgh, Scotland court ruled that texting in sick—specifically after the death of a loved one—is not sufficient grounds for dismissal.

The town of Deltona, Florida banned texting during town meetings, while Dutch government employees are prohibited from using Wikipedia.

One English company banned internal email as a way to encourage employees to actually speak to each other.

Say What?

Employees at a Welsh company face fines for using the words, "recession," "economic crisis," or "credit crisis." The company directors said the measure was meant to maintain a positive atmosphere.

A German company has an anti-whining law. Anyone caught complaining can be fired on the spot.

The town of Harrow banned the use of jargon in town meetings and documents. Words like "incentivizing," "place shaping," "holistic," and "synergies" will no longer be used. Jargon was also banned by the Local Government Association in the UK.

Break Room Blues

The Liverpool city council voted to do away with water coolers in city offices.

Making microwave popcorn at work may soon be against the law for employees of the city of Seattle. Burnt microwave popcorn triggered fire alarms and forced the evacuation of the city's Justice Center and Municipal Tower one too many times.

Two employees of Yellowstone National Park were fired for urinating into Old Faithful.

Man, you really had to go.

Overtime

The town council of South El Monte, California passed a law prohibiting its mayor from working past 11:00 P.M. at night because they were worried about her staying in the building so late and exhausting herself.

How to Get Out of Work

In South Carolina, "Any employee of any business which operates on Sunday under the provisions of this section has the option of refusing to work in accordance with Section 53-1-100. Any employer who dismisses or demotes an employee because he is a conscientious objector to Sunday work is subject to a civil penalty of treble the damages found by the court or the jury plus court costs and the employee's attorney's fees. The court may order the employer to rehire or reinstate the employee in the same position he was in prior to dismissal or demotion without forfeiture of compensation, rank, or grade."

Not in Front of the Children

A Florida teacher was fired for performing magic tricks for his class. A parent accused him of wizardry.

In a small British town, a school employee was sacked for punching a parent in the face while on a field trip.

Questionable Professions

Fortune-tellers are prohibited from practicing in Natchez, Mississippi according to a 1954 law. Specifically included in the ban are: reading tea leaves, reading palms, astrology, and "all other forms of fortune-telling."

In Livingston Parish, Louisiana, "soothsaying" is against the law. In many US cities, fortune-telling is allowed only with a permit.

In Houma, Louisiana, it's illegal for barbers to cut hair on a Sunday or Monday. In Italy, there's an old superstition that

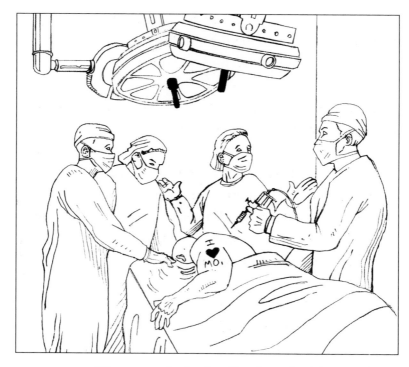

*Nurse, now look what I've done. I said
pass me the black, not the pink!*

the best time for a haircut is while the moon is full. But cutting hair by the light of the moon is against the law. All salons must be closed by 7 P.M.

A man in Ohio was arrested for cutting grass at a public park because he was not a contractor for or employee of the city. He just thought the grass needed cutting.

Until very recently, it was illegal to offer tattoo services in Massachusetts unless you were a medical doctor.

FRAUD ON THE COURT

Sports and games are based on rules, and there are a lot of them. They extend beyond how a game is played to what players can wear while playing and even whether or not the game came be played in the first place. And then there are the fans. More often than not, they're the ones who just don't seem to know how to play by the rules.

105

Out of Bounds

"Flaming football" is illegal in the US. The game, which originated in Australia, consists of a small ball that's dipped in kerosene and then set on fire. Participants then kick the ball around. The winner, presumably, is the one who does not receive third-degree burns. The ball was available online for a cost of $35. Australia also banned the game after a teenager was seriously burned.

Aluminum baseball bats are prohibited in the state of New York.

Alcohol is not a banned substance at track and field events, but one Russian high jumper was suspended from future competitions for showing up drunk on vodka and Red Bull at an international meet.

The little-known but much loved sport of donkey ball is

My wife told me to get off my ass and get some exercise.

against the law in Oregon, New Jersey, Ohio, and Pennsylvania. Never heard of it? Well, in this game, participants try to dunk baskets on a basketball court with regulation-height nets, while mounted on donkeys.

Irish soldiers deployed on a peacekeeping mission to Chad were prohibited from playing soccer and volleyball in order to prevent them from getting injured.

Non-Regulation Dress

The "mankini" a tiny, Speedo-style bathing suit worn by men stretched up from the groin and over the shoulders has been banned in England's Wembley Stadium and at other venues and events including the New Zealand rugby championships. The garment, made famous by Borat, the character played by British comedian Sasha Baron Cohen, became popular with male fans, but officials say it's not appropriate attire for events where children will be present.

Players from an Illinois high school basketball team were barred from competing in a state semifinal game because of a technical foul. They had a non-regulation stripe on their uniforms. According to state rules, side stripes must be vertically centered below the armpit and no more than four inches wide. The team's uniform featured stripes that curled around the armpits.

Forget steroids. The world of competitive swimming is focusing on another unfair advantage—high-tech swimsuits, which critics say amount to "technological doping." The international swimming organization FINA has banned from competition, swimsuits that cover the neck, shoulders, or ankles, and which exceed a certain level of thickness and buoyancy. In 2009, when 108 world records were broken, 79 of the swimmers were wearing the Speedo LZR Racer suit. While that suit will still be legal, other suits, which trap air bubbles and compress the body won't be. Officials say that the rules will keep swimming a sport that focuses on the athlete's performance instead of their gear.

Smells Like Team Spirit

A Wisconsin high school outlawed a number of cheers because they were thought to express unsportsmanlike conduct. The ousted cheers include: "Nah nah nah nah, hey hey hey goodbye," "Overrated," and "What's the Score?" Fans are also prohibited from booing at an official's call, screaming during a foul shot, or throwing things at the playing field. Penalties include being kicked out of the game or being suspended from school.

National Football League cheerleaders are prohibited from "warming up" outside of the opposing team's locker rooms.

Fan Bans

Cambodian Buddhist monks are allowed to watch World

Cup soccer games on television, but they are required to "remain passive" while watching and can face defrocking if they cheer or express emotion. They are also prohibited from betting on games or watching them in public.

In the state of Washington, fans at school games are prohibited from booing.

A pair of drunken University of Wisconsin fans (not students at the school) were banned from the stadium for having sex in the bathroom. The couple tried to persuade the officer that they were only going to the bathroom in the same stall, but one finally admitted the infraction.

Male fans may not attend the women's cricket championship in Pakistan as spectators.

Fans of the Scottish soccer team the Rangers were banned

from singing "The Hokey Cokey" (known in some other countries as "The Hokey Pokey) at a game against a rival team, the Celtics. The song, which is frequently sung at children's parties, apparently has roots in the Puritan ear, and was used to mock Catholics. Officials said that a fan dispute, which grew on an online forum, had led to the association of the song with anti-Catholic sentiments and would therefore be religiously threatening to Celtic fans. Officials stated that anyone caught singing the song at the game could be charged with a hate crime. Fans were also recently threatened with arrest if they sang the "Famine Song," another song considered to be anti-Irish and anti-Catholic.

Where's That Kid's Birth Certificate?
A nine-year old pitcher in Connecticut was banned from his baseball league for being too good. Officials say his fastball, which reached up to 40 mph, threatened injuries. There are

Are you sure that kid's nine?

now more lawyers on the field than players.

A nine-year-old Australian girl was banned from playing at her local tennis club for excessive grunting.

The British Are Coming!

The behavior of British soccer fans is notorious in Europe. Fans of the Liverpool team were blamed for the 1985 collapse of a stadium wall in Belgium, which left thirty-nine Italian fans dead. Continual riots left the government so embarrassed that in 2000 it passed the Football Disorder Act. The act allows the government to ban offenders from entering playing fields at home or abroad. The worst offenders have been banned from leaving the UK and ordered to turn in their passports while English teams are playing overseas. It's not just the British government that has banned its own fans. In countries where British football teams play, including Spain, Germany, Italy and Portugal, local authorities have banned fans of English teams from entering their city centers. In their defense, fans say failure in crowd control and police brutality contribute to many of the fan riots that take place on foreign soil.

The British aren't the only offenders by far. Fans of the Italian soccer team Juventus were even banned from going to their home stadium as a penalty for some fans' racist chants against a rival team member. Fans of Napoli's team were prevented from traveling to away games after nonpaying fans crowded trains, slashed train seats, and set off fireworks in the train causing over $500,000 in damages.

The fan bans even reach high school levels. Fans from a visiting school's team are prohibited from attending varsity boys' basketball games in Chicago after violence continually erupted after games.

Buy Me Some Crackerjacks?

Peanuts have been banned from a special enclosed section of Camden Yards in Baltimore. The twenty-five-seat section is intended to allow fans with peanut allergies to enjoy watching a game without fear of airborne contagions.

After recess, the officers broke up a huge
lunch-money laundering ring.

Dodging the Rules

Dodgeball has been outlawed in elementary schools in Maine, Maryland, New York, Virginia, Texas, Massachusetts, and Utah. One district in Maryland banned any game with "human targets."

HOUSE ARREST

Some laws hit you where you live, literally. There are laws to regulate lawns and gardens, doormats and clotheslines. And that doesn't even count the draconian measures imposed upon your kitchen sink.

Home Improvements?

The town of Bristol, England banned welcome mats because they're a tripping hazard. The ban however was later overturned.

In Atlanta, Georgia and Austin, Texas, it's against the law to build a ginormous new McMansion on a postage-stamp lot after you've torn down the old ranch house that once sat on the property.

In Minnesota, bathtubs are required to have feet. But in Missouri, installing a bathtub with legs resembling animal paws is prohibited.

In Kanata, Ontario, house and garage colors are regulated by city laws. Homeowners can be fined for a bright orange door. Meanwhile, a group of neighbors in Sequim, Washington petitioned the local tax authority to lower their property taxes because they said a neighbor's purple paint job drove their property values down.

It's against the law to install a garbage disposal in your sink or repair a broken one in Raleigh, North Carolina. The infraction carries a $25,000 per day fine or a lifetime ban on the use of city water. Officials say the device leads to over-flowing sewage in city waterways.

A homebuyer in Arizona sued the person she bought her house from, demanding that he take back the home because it was purchased under false pretenses. The seller, it seems, failed to reveal that he had called the police on the neighbors hundreds of times for infractions including throwing potatoes at the home just days before it was purchased. Arizona law requires that a seller disclose such information.

The Tiniest Zoning Commission in the World?

In Iceland, building projects must first be cleared by the little people. New construction projects can only take place in areas that are known not to be inhabited by elves. A local elf communicator will be consulted to see whether or not the supernatural beings would be disturbed by the project. In the 1970s, a road construction project was altered because

*. . . And all the doorknobs have to come down
at least another eighteen inches.*

elves were believed to live in nearby rocks. Elves can also make their feelings known by messing with equipment so it doesn't function. If this happens, it's considered to be a message that the project shouldn't go forward.

Don't Put Another Log on the Fire

In the town of Hampstead, Quebec installing a new woodstove in your home is prohibited, and residents have seven years to remove their existing woodstoves. (The law doesn't, however, include fireplaces or outdoor barbeques.) The mayor of the town says the law is intended to prevent pollution and that wood fire smoke is similar to cigarette smoking in its adverse effects on health and the environment. Montreal is planning a similar ban, and one is being considered in the San Francisco Bay area.

Garden Variety Crimes

A homeowner in Buffalo, New York was ticketed for sight

obstruction when his sunflowers grew seventeen feet tall and blocked the view exiting his driveway.

In Canton, Ohio residents must keep their grass cut to between four and six inches or face stiff penalties, including potential fines and jail time.

A man in St. Petersburg, Florida was jailed for having a brown lawn, in violation of his homeowner's association covenant.

A Laundry List of Offenses

It's illegal to do laundry after midnight in Brooklyn, New York.

In London, you can't hang laundry out across a street.

Clotheslines were banned in Ontario briefly until public outcry caused a repeal of the ban. However, an estimated 30 million Americans do not have the right to dry their clothes outside due to homeowner's association regulations.

In the domestic battery department: In London, it's illegal to beat or shake carpets after 8 A.M.

Holiday Spirit
In San Diego, you could be ticketed for leaving your Christmas lights on your home past February. In Aurora, Illinois, you have sixty days after putting them up to remove them. In Minnesota, you only have until January 14th.

A man in Paisley, England called his neighbors "killjoys" after they joined together to have his 8,000 Christmas lights put out. In Berkshire, England a man who regularly used up to 22,000 Christmas lights in addition to various inflatable decorations was forced to scale back his display. One California man—whose display included a fifty-foot-tall tree and 50,000 lights—was required to get a special event permit for his holiday display because it drew thousands of visitors to the neighborhood. Another California household erected a custom-made ten-foot-tall Grinch in its yard after complaining neighbors shut down their extensive Christmas display. The Grinch came complete with a loud recording that played "You're a Mean One, Mr. Grinch" again and again on a loop.

Abominable Snowmen

An Alaska family was ordered to remove their sixteen-foot-tall snowman Snowzilla after officials said the friendly-looking snow sculpture drew too many crowds to the neighborhood and caused road hazards. The following year, the banned snowman "mysteriously" reappeared on the property, bigger than ever at twenty-five feet tall.

Two men in Cincinnati were arrested for attacking an inflatable yard snowman with a screwdriver.

Outdoor Living Room

In Murfreesboro, Tennessee and Lincoln, Nebraska it's illegal to place indoor furniture outdoors. In Pittsburgh, Pennsylvania, the law is limited to sofas and mattresses. In each location, authorities say the law is intended to encourage people to actually take rotten, old, rat-infested furniture to the dump instead of leaving it in the yard.

Taking It to the Streets

In Brooklyn, New York, it's against the law to hose the sidewalk in the morning.

Homeowners in Gananoque, Ontario are responsible for clearing the snow off the city sidewalks in front of their homes.

Homeowner's Associations Gone Mad!

A homeowner in Georgia was cited for having an illegal fence, which was actually built by the development company issuing the citation.

In a separate Georgia development, a homeowner was cited for leaving her blinds up during the day.

A Texas homeowner's association banned pickup trucks from the neighborhood's driveways.

A Colorado homeowner's association cited a resident for a peace-sign shaped Christmas wreath and threatened to impose a $25-a-day fine until it was removed.

Driveway Moments

In Washington, DC, homeowners can be ticketed for parking in their driveways if they don't pull in far enough.

In many cities, such as Colombia, South Carolina and Houston, Texas, vehicles can't be parked on lawns in city limits. On the other hand, in metro New York, homeowners can't pave over their entire front yard to turn it into a parking lot.

In one Texas town, it's against the law to park in front of someone else's house at night.

FOR CROWN AND COUNTRY

Love of one's country is a very passionate thing. But it's important not to get too carried away and, say, start waltzing while your national anthem is being played or wearing a bikini emblazoned with your country's flag. Love of your native language is important, too. But using too many foreign words might corrupt your mother tongue and lead to who knows what. Perhaps most importantly, no matter where in the world you live or come from, it's imperative that the corrupting influence of Bart and Homer Simpson be stopped from spreading any further in the world than it already has.

Patriotic Duty

In Thailand, traffic must come to a complete stop while the national anthem is being played. This happens twice a day.

In the UK, it's illegal to waltz to the national anthem. It's illegal to dance while the national anthem is being played in several US states. A US baseball fan was ejected by stadium security for leaving the stands to go to the bathroom during the national anthem. Desecration of the national anthem (such as using it in a mash-up) is against the law in Russia. Russian men are also required by law to remove their hats while it's being played.

In Turkey, it is against the law to insult Kemal Ataturk, the founder of the country. It is also illegal to speak unfavorably about the present-day president of the country.

Election Year Politics

In Japan, politicians are not allowed to use Twitter during their campaigns. City council members in Cincinnati are not permitted to tweet during council meetings. The decision, which stirred citywide debate, came after a council member made remarks about another council member's speech on her Twitter account while council was in session. While the member argued that council meetings are open to the public, colleagues argued that the technology was distracting them from business at hand.

When a nineteen-year old nearly won the mayoral election in the small Ohio town of Streetsboro, the (considerably older) city council members decided to impose a minimum age of twenty-three on all candidates running for public office in the town.

The council member's tweeting had his colleagues all a flutter.

Locals Only

It's illegal to be foreign in the city of Norlisk, Russia.

Holland is considering a law that would ban foreigners from its famed cannabis coffee houses. People come from all over the world to legally smoke pot in public in the Netherlands. But one of the country's political parties argued that the foreign "drug tourists" were too unruly.

Foreigners are not allowed to buy gas in Malaysia. When gas prices go up, people in neighboring countries used to flock to Malaysian border towns to buy it at a subsidized rate.

At least one-third of all the content aired on Canadian radio stations must be Canadian.

Foreigners who "show disrespect" towards Russia while there can be kicked out or denied entry.

Foreigners are not permitted in China's spy museum.

Cambodia recently lifted a ban on Cambodian women marrying foreigners.

The town of Laverkin, Utah declared itself a "UN-free" zone, and outlawed the flying of the UN flag and doing business with the UN or any contractors who do.

Waving the Flag (or Not)

In Brazil, it's illegal to wear a Brazilian-flag-patterned bikini.

In Pahrump, Nevada, it's against the law to fly a foreign flag. The law came about because citizens in the town objected to Mexican immigrants flying the Mexican flag during an immigration law protest.

In North Dakota, foreign flags can be displayed as long as

they are the flags of friendly foreign nations.

In New Jersey, a foreign flag may be displayed as long as it's accompanied by a US flag of equal dimension.

A teacher in Colorado was arrested for displaying the flags of foreign countries in his classroom as part of his geography curriculum. Foreign flags are also not allowed in schools in Rhode Island.

While it's not illegal to have an American flag tattoo, a man in Melbourne, Florida was prevented from having his city's seal tattooed on his arm. The man's request for permission to recreate the seal on his arm was denied by the city manager, in part because of a state law that restricts use of city seals to city documents. Infractions of the law are punishable by a $500 fine or up to sixty days in jail. The man said he loves his city, and just wanted the tattoo to show his pride.

The Mother Tongue

In 2008, the Iranian president kicked all foreign words out of the Persian language.

In the city of Kunming, China, foreign place names are against the law. City officials took the measure to stop the proliferation of apartment building names such as "French Gardens" or "Paris of the East."

France has banned imported techie words such as "email," "blog," and "post box" from its language.

So Long, Simpsons

In China, foreign animated cartoons are not allowed during primetime viewing.

In Venezuela, the Simpsons in particular have been banned from being shown at all.

Natural
Law

SOME believe laws are what separate us from the animals. Others believe we need laws to separate us from animals. Still others believe we are what we eat, but others believe that there ought to be laws against what most people eat. Like it or not, we live and die by the law (as you'll soon see in the Wrongful Death section). It's survival of the fittest: or of those who have the best lawyers.

TOXIC TORT

Regulating all the food and drink we consume is no piece of cake. Lawmakers faced with this task often come up with some pretty creative and unusual ways to save us from bad food . . . and ourselves.

No Approval for Seal

Once considered "Antarctic delicacies," seal brain, grilled cormorant, and penguin breast and eggs have been banned from Antarctic research stations. While station chefs used to come up with creative recipes for fresh wildlife—such as seal brain au gratin and brain fritters—they must now rely on food shipped in twice a year.

Out of the Oven . . .

It's legal to eat road kill in West Virginia, Tennessee, and North Carolina as long as you're the one who killed it and are not simply poaching off a kill someone else ran over and left behind.

In Hawaii, it is illegal to cook food in lava.

In New Jersey, you're not allowed to slurp soup in a public restaurant. Violators are subject to a fine, arrest, and potential jail time.

It's against the law to serve coffee, tea, or any food in a

funeral home in New York or New Jersey.

Bringing pork products into Yemen could result in the death penalty.

Yes, We Have No Bananas

A school in Plymouth, England banned kids from bringing bananas to school with lunch because a teacher at the school had a potentially fatal allergy to them. The school stated it would lift the ban once the teacher was no longer at the school. That's not the only banana ban in the UK, though. A former law prohibited the sale of "bendy" bananas, "knobby" carrots and cucumbers, and other fruit and vegetables that didn't conform to EU (European Union) standards. The law—called the "straight fruit law" by some—required that all fruit and vegetables sold for consumption must be straight and not in any unusual form. Fruit or vegetables not conforming to the standard could only be used in processed

Where bad fruit goes to get straightened out.

food. The ban was lifted after several years of enforcement.

Beware the Pizza Police
In Italy, not just any pizza can bear the name Neapolitan.

There are strict rules for maintaining pizza purity. The dough must be soft, elastic, not sticky, and be left to rest for at least six hours. It must be kneaded and shaped by hand. Rolling pins or other mechanical instruments are not permitted. The pizza must be no more than 35 centimeters (14 inches) in diameter and no thicker than a ⅓ centimeter (.1 inch) in the center, and the crust must rise to 2 centimeters (.8 inch). It must be cooked in a wood-fired oven. There are only three approved recipes: Marinara with garlic and oregano; Margherita, with basil, tomatoes, and cheese; and Extra Margherita, which includes buffalo mozzarella.

The city of Lucca, Italy outlawed couscous, kebabs, and curries from being sold in the city's restaurants as a measure to preserve the authenticity of local cuisine. It's also illegal to snack on the steps of Italian churches or in front of famous monuments such as the Trevi Fountain or the Spanish Steps in Rome.

The Pennsylvania Pie Incident

It seemed like the most innocent thing on Earth: a bunch of Catholic grannies selling their home-baked pies at the Friday Lenten fish fry at their church. But things are never truly what they seem. These sweet little old ladies were brazenly breaking a Pennsylvania statute: Any institution that sells food four times a year or more must get a temporary food and beverage license, and the food sold must be prepared in a kitchen that has passed state inspection. A state inspector, who just happened to be doing his rounds when the pies arrived, declared the pies illegal for sale, breaking the hearts of hungry parishioners and depriving the church of the $1 per slice revenue it would have made from the sales. According to the law, the ladies could continue to sell their home-baked pies if they paid a $35 fee and had their kitchens inspected. "Piegate"—as the incident came to be known—ended happily, with a local bakery donating pies for the event. A state senator later drafted a resolution to overturn the law.

Got the Munchies?

Marijuana-flavored candy is now against the law in Chicago; Suffolk County, New York; Michigan; New Jersey; and Pennsylvania. Concerned lawmakers feared that the confection—sold at music festivals, convenience stores, and head shops—would fall into the hands of children who would then develop a taste for the illicit substance.

No Waist? No Service

A Mississippi lawmaker introduced legislation that would ban restaurants from serving food to obese people. The state would provide restaurants with criteria for determining who was obese. Repeat infractions would lead to the restaurant's license being suspended. Mississippi has the highest rate of obesity in the US. The legislation was withdrawn before it went to a vote.

McDonald's Happy Meals are prohibited in Liverpool, England. City officials say the measure was passed in an effort to combat childhood obesity.

A federal prosecutor in Brazil has introduced a measure to ban toys that accompany fast-food kids' meals because they "create emotional associations" between the junk food and the satisfaction of getting a free surprise.

I Can't Believe It's Not Butter

Hiding in plain sight, right there in Missouri's dairy cases is an illicit substance, once banned across the world from Australia to Canada: margarine. This smooth and (arguably) tasty bread spreader was once considered the biggest threat to the world's dairy farmers. And they made every effort to stamp it out. For almost 100 years, the "oleo wars" as the butter-margarine fracas came to be known, raged in places from Quebec to Queensland. But nowhere was the battle fiercer than in America's Dairyland: Wisconsin. Until 1967, it was illegal for restaurants and public institutions in Wisconsin to serve margarine. It was illegal for margarine to be colored yellow: that might lead unsuspecting citizens to believe that it was real butter. Missouri is the last holdout in the oleo wars, but there are still some other weird butter laws on the books. In Alabama, it's illegal to make or sell "renovated butter," a product made from old, yucky butter that's melted with new butter.

Junk Food Justice

In Waltham Forest near London, it's illegal to sell junk food within 400 meters of a school.

It's against the law to serve food with more than half a gram of trans fat per serving in New York restaurants.

In California, cupcakes and cookies can't be sold at school bake sales because their sugar and fat content exceeds the

Masters of the obvious.

recommended content for food sold during school hours.

Liquid Assets

Forget the bans on junk food. Drinking one of the world's most pure and natural substances is against the law in twenty-eight US states. Raw, unpasteurized milk is illegal for human consumption, although it can be purchased as "pet milk" for animals. In 2008, a horse-and-buggy-driving Amish farmer was arrested on his Pennsylvania farm for delivering his contraband milk across state lines to natural food lovers in New York.

In the UK, milk bottles must contain the following warning: Contains Milk.

An artichoke beverage that was said to "eliminate alcohol from the body six times faster than your normal metabolism" was banned from France because authorities said it did not live up to its claims. The makers of the beverage claimed that authorities were just trying to prevent people from using it to dodge drinking and driving laws.

The Hoagie Defense?

A Florida man was arrested for domestic battery after throwing a sandwich in his girlfriend's face.

A Shelbyville, Tennessee couple was arrested and held on $2,500 bond after they got into a war of words and then "attacked" each other with a bag of Cheetos. Although neither was hurt in the attack, both were charged with domestic assault.

Dog Gone

In Los Angeles, California, it's illegal for street vendors to sell bacon-wrapped hot dogs unless they are sold from a specially designed cart that costs $26,000. Health inspectors have

*The dispute would have lasted longer, but Darryl
got the munchies and ate the ammunition.*

classified bacon as a potentially harmful substance because it must be stored at exactly the right temperature or it could lead to bacteria and illness. Violators of the law risk immediate confiscation and destruction of their bacon, and can be fined up to $1,000 or face up to six months in jail. The demand for bacon dogs remains so high, however, that some vendors take the risk and secretly offer the snack to those who ask. One such vendor spent forty-five days in prison.

CREATURES OF STATUTE

The law of the jungle may not apply to humans, but humans do have some pretty strange laws about their interactions with animals. Sometimes, it seems humans need the law to prevent them from behaving like animals.

Completely Nuts

Laws are frequently made to protect the most vulnerable in our society: the powerless squirrel, for example. Thankfully, it's illegal to "molest" squirrels in any way in Minnesota. You also can't sell them in Vermont or hunt them by means of falconry in Georgia (except during the summer). In Connecticut, it's illegal to hunt squirrels with dynamite,

Nuts! You've got to be kidding me!

sulfur gas, or "brimstone" (that substance that, they say, is found in quantity in hell).

As if the odor that would result from doing so were not enough to prevent you from doing so . . . it's illegal to tease a skunk in Minnesota.

In the UK, it's against the law to disturb a badger while it's occupying its lair or to possess or control a dead badger.

It's illegal to get an elephant drunk in Natchez, Mississippi. The law stems from an early nineteenth-century resident of the city who had a live elephant show at his home. Someone at the show apparently gave the elephant a beer. Things got so out of hand that legal action was required.

In England, it's illegal to post a "Beware of Dog" sign where there is no dog to beware of.

The states of Florida and Washington have outlawed fish pedicures: a spa procedure during which the client puts his or her feet into a basin of small flesh-eating carp called *garra rupa*, which eat away at the dead skin, leaving feet smooth and soft. Regulators claim that there isn't enough evidence that the procedure is sanitary.

Having a hamster as a pet is against the law in Vietnam.

The Traffic Is Beastly

You can drive sheep down Hollywood Boulevard in Los Angeles, as long as you have fewer than 2,000.

During amphibian migration season in Independence, New Jersey, frogs and salamanders have the right of way at "amphibian crossing" sites. Human crossing guards stop traffic and help the critters get across the road in bucket brigades.

You should see the crowd—they're flocking to see us.
I thought I saw Ba-a-a-abra Streisand on line!

And yes, you know this had to be on the books somewhere: In Quitman, Georgia, it's illegal for chickens to cross the road. Now, if only the joke, and all of its fowl offshoots could be outlawed.

Rules of the Chase

It's illegal to hunt from a moving vehicle in Louisiana, Colorado, California, and Arkansas. In Oregon, that includes dirt bikes. It is, however, legal to shoot wolves from a helicopter in Alaska.

You can hunt from a boat in Hungary, as long as the boat is powered by oars and there are no more than two people and one dog in the boat.

In Ontario, you can moose hunt from a motorboat as long as the motor is turned off, the boat is anchored, and there are no whitecaps on the water.

Animal Attraction

Animals aren't allowed to mate near a house of worship in California. They're not even allowed to do the deed within city limits in Minnesota.

Authorities in the Saudi capital of Riyadh noticed a disturbing trend. Men were using their dog-walking routines to make advances toward women—a big no-no in this strict Islamic society. Now it's against the law for pets to be exercised in public places.

A Royal Catch

According to a statute from the time of King Edward II (he reigned from 1307 to 1327), whales, porpoises, and sturgeons are considered "royal fish" in the UK, and fishermen must offer their hauls of these species to the Crown. In 2004, the auction of nine-foot-long, 264-pound sturgeon caught in Swansea Bay ended with the mysterious disappearance of the fish just after the Devon and Cornwall police (tipped off by an insider) showed up at the auction and took pictures of it. Following the law, the fisherman had contacted the Receiver of the Wrecks, who faxed Buckingham Palace and offered it to the Queen. Her office politely declined. With the go-ahead from the Crown, he decided to auction it off, and the fish went for the princely sum of £650 ($1,500). But selling the fish is also against the law, carrying a fine of £5,000 ($8,300) or six months in prison. After questioning the auctioneer about "what the fish was wearing when it disappeared," the police later recovered the missing fish, holding it at an undisclosed location until it was transferred to the Natural History Museum. The fisherman and the auctioneer were let off the hook.

The Right to Arm Wrestle Bears?

Bear wrestling: the act of a human and a bear engaging in a wrestling match in front of an audience. While in some areas this "sport" requires an explanation, in others, it's so rampant that it had to be outlawed. Those areas include Louisiana, Alabama, and Oklahoma.

In London, it's understandably against the law to "keep a

room or pit for the purpose of baiting lions."

It's illegal to steal an alligator (alive or dead) in Louisiana. Doing so can get you up to ten years in prison or a $3,000 fine. It's also against the law to steal a crawfish in the state.

It's against the law to sell an armadillo in Texas (when it's still alive).

You Lookin' at Me?

Staring at the apes is against the law at the Antwerp zoo. Zookeepers say that the ban was enacted because too much eye contact leads the animals to isolate themselves and lose their social skills.

No Freeloading, Tax-Dodging Cats on Federal Property!

In 2008, an orange tabby named Sammy was evicted from

his home at the post office of Notasulga, Alabama, population 843. His crime? That freeloading feline was living on federal property, and yet he had never paid a dime in taxes! After a local resident complained, the postmaster was obliged to kick him out. A group of concerned citizens, however, pooled their resources to rent the cat a post office box so that he would have a valid excuse to hang out and nap in the window.

Afowl of the Law

In Minnesota, "no chick, duckling, gosling, or rabbit that has been dyed or otherwise colored artificially may be sold or offered for sale; raffled; offered or given as a prize, premium, or advertising device; or displayed in any store, shop, carnival, or other public place."

In Kentucky it's illegal to sell chicks, ducklings, or goslings that have been dyed, but it's also illegal to dye them unless they are over two months old.

Uncle Earl Is Above the Law

Hog-dog fights (that's a fight between a dog and a "swine, hog, boar, or pig") are illegal in Mississippi, Florida, South Carolina, Tennessee, and Alabama. In Louisiana, canine and hog fighting is against the law except for Uncle Earl's Hog Dog Trials, owing to it being a heritage event and all.

Greasy pig contests are against the law in Rhode Island and Minnesota. Chicken and turkey scrambles are also verboten in Minnesota.

Possession of a Toad with Intent to Lick

So far, owning a Sonoran Desert or Colorado River toad is not illegal in the US per se. But in 2007, one Kansas City, Missouri man got in trouble with the law for possession with intent to lick the little critter. You see, the innocent-looking

Don't even think about it.

frog is actually a delivery system for bufotenine, a controlled hallucinogenic substance that it carries in its glands. Licking the toad is said to produce a high, but some people say it's a better trip if you milk the toad's glands, and then dry out and smoke the venom.

In Australia, the much maligned cane toad—an invasive species that has run rampant in Queensland—is said to have similar qualities. Tales of "Australian hippies" smoking cane toad venom became a media sensation in the late 1980s, but the practice was never outlawed. The cane toad is, however, the subject of another Australian law: It's illegal to bring a cane toad into Western Australian.

CRIMES AGAINST NATURE

Stop right there. Step away from the pine needles. Raking up that worthless substance can get you a fine or even jail time (if you're on someone else's property in North Carolina).

And don't even think of picking up that chunk of lava from Hawaii Volcanoes National Park. Not only will a park ranger ticket you, but the goddess of the volcano will curse you with bad luck. Bottom line: don't mess with Mother Nature. Or at least don't mess with the laws made to protect her.

Rain, Rain, Go Away

It's illegal to harvest rainwater in Utah. Lawmakers say that capturing the rainwater means there is less to go around for others who might live downstream and that some people actually collect rainwater to sell it (which would mean they would owe taxes on it).

Aaargh! It's the Eco-Pirates

In an effort to stem public water contamination, Spokane, Washington became the first city to ban the sale and use of high-phosphorous dishwasher detergent, which can get into lakes and streams, killing fish and destroying ecosystems.

Residents may purchase eco-friendly detergents with a lower concentration of potentially dangerous chemicals; however, some report that they feel that the "green" cleaners just don't get their dishes as clean. Some have taken to crossing the border into neighboring Idaho to purchase the detergent and "smuggling" it back into Spokane. Border-town supermarkets in Idaho report a 10% increase in their dishwasher detergent sales since the ban began. Canada and several US states are considering similar bans against phosphates.

A region of Peru was the first place on Earth to outlaw bio-piracy. Bio-piracy is a term used to describe the practice of corporations collecting plants used by indigenous peoples as traditional medicines and then patenting that knowledge and using it for their own purposes. (All of this without compensating or sharing the financial gains with the indigenous people, of course.) The law requires that companies must now seek permission from the local people for using their knowledge and compensate them if they have any financial gain from its use.

Wacky Weeds

In Oklahoma, Missouri, Tennessee, Louisiana, Delaware, and Maine, a weed that's found commonly growing on the sides of roads is now illegal. Jimson weed, which is also sometimes called mad hatter, stink weed, loco weed, green dragon, and zombie cucumber, grows wild in many areas of the Eastern US. Historical accounts say that British soldiers, attempting to quell a colonial rebellion in Jamestown in 1676, ingested the weed (either accidentally or by means of sabotage). They were later seen chasing feathers, sitting naked, and kissing each other. The soldiers were easily overcome by the colonists. Since current-day teens found out that Jimson weed seeds can be chewed, smoked, or made into tea, and are said to have hallucinogenic effects, use of the weed as a drug has grown.

The Duchess of Northumberland was granted a permit to grow cannabis, "magic mushrooms," opium poppies, and other plants from which illegal drugs are derived for a poison garden cultivated for educational purposes. (Yeah, right . . . educational purposes, my foot.)

The Wildflower Mafia

Law enforcement officials in England say that the theft of wild plant bulbs has become a thriving black market business and believe that organized crime is involved. Bluebells, snowdrops, weft-forming moss, and orchids have been stolen from wild protected sites and private property at an alarming rate. They have a high market value—a single snowdrop bulb can sell for up to £45 ($75). One bluebell thief was jailed for four months for stealing 1,300 protected bluebell bulbs in Norfolk. Officials say that competitive plant brokers have hired organized gangs to trade in their switchblades for trowels and do the thieving for them.

Pollen Police

In Albuquerque, New Mexico, it's illegal to sell, cultivate, or plant pollen-producing trees. Selling elms, cypresses, mulberries, or male junipers more than 2 feet tall is punishable by a fine of up to $500. Tucson and Phoenix, Arizona; Las Vegas, Nevada; and El Paso, Texas have similar bans.

Nuisance plants (those that threaten the area's aesthetic, environmental, wildlife, or recreational benefits) are against the law in Delaware and several other states and municipalities.

In North Carolina, it's against the law to place poisonous shrubs or vegetable plants in public places. It's also against the law to collect the endangered Venus flytrap, a rare carnivorous plant that grows in the area. Plant poachers generally only face small fines, but a Dutch citizen attempting to smuggle 9,000 flytrap seedlings out of the country was recently held on $50,000 bond.

In Connecticut and New Hampshire, it's illegal to sell the popular landscaping shrubs barberry or burning bush. While these plants are commonly found in nurseries and home centers all over the US, they're invasive species, and could potentially start to push out the state's native plants. A few types of barberry are illegal in Canada.

In Pennsylvania, it's illegal to move the state plant—the mountain laurel—from a position where it grows naturally. Most national parks prohibit picking wildflowers or native plants. Contrary to popular belief, it's not illegal to pick bluebonnets in Texas.

In drought-plagued Palm Desert, California, it's tough to keep greenery growing. While the city successfully grew potted palms and plants, poaching from public places became such a problem that in addition security cameras, the city installed microchips in the plants to track down thieves.

Plant poachers face fines and other penalties. Microchips are also being used to protect rare ginseng in Mammoth Cave National Park and saguaro cacti in Saguaro National Park among other public places.

Collection Fees

It's against the law to write or draw big letters or pictures in the sand on the Tottori Dunes on Japan's coast. Creating "dune graffiti" featuring letters or pictures measuring more than 10 square meters is punishable by fines of up to 50,000 yen ($525). Local officials say that the wide open spaces inspired some tourists to etch unusually large messages of love or pictures into the sand, distracting from the area's "natural beauty" and ruining the experience for others.

It's illegal to forage for food in New York City parks without a permit. In the UK, it's illegal to forage on National Trust lands, Nature Reserves, or land owned by the military. In Los

That's gonna cost you!

Angeles, all fruit or vegetables that grow over a sidewalk are considered to be public and therefore can be legally eaten.

Florida treasure hunters were fined $589,311 for destroying

sea grass while treasure hunting without a permit. The grass covered over one acre and will take 50 to 100 years to grow back.

In North Carolina, you can be charged for the crime of pine needle larceny—raking or removing pine needles with intent to steal.

Up a Tree

Tree sitting—the practice of occupying a tree so that it won't be felled by a timber company is illegal in the US and Canada, because it's considered trespassing.

WRONGFUL DEATH

With death being such a sensitive topic, it's not surprising that there a lot of laws to deal with what to do when it happens. Some are perfectly reasonable of course, others will almost make you die of laughter.

The Big Chill

The town of Nederland, Colorado banned cryogenics (the practice of generating extremely cold temperatures that can prevent a corpse from decomposing), making it a nuisance to keep frozen bodies on your property. The law was enacted in response to a local family (including an aspiring cryogenicist) who was keeping the body of a relative and another man on dry ice in town. The law was later repealed. To complicate matters, the family was deported back to their native Norway and had to leave the bodies behind in fear that they would thaw in transport. The bodies are now interned in a structure called the Tuffshed Cryogenic Mausoleum, which is taken care of by the town and has become a local tourist attraction. The town even holds an annual Frozen Dead Guy Day featuring a coffin race and a Grim Reaper parade. When a cryogenically frozen French couple was deemed illegal in France, the town of Nederland offered to take them in.

Unfortunately the town's "Dead Guy in the Fridge" event failed to draw a large enough crowd.

173

Dead Wrong

Taxicabs in London are forbidden from carrying corpses.

In British Columbia, it's illegal to kill Sasquatch (as Bigfoot is called in that area) should you actually encounter him . . . her . . . it.

At funerals at Australian Catholic churches, it's forbidden to mention drunkenness or sex in a eulogy. Eulogies are also limited to five minutes. At Catholic funerals in Ireland, no music composed especially for the deceased, recitation of favorite poems, or singing of favorite songs is allowed.

The diocese of Bath and Wells in England banned garden gnomes on graves because they are "unnatural creatures." Church officials cited the teddy bears and plastic flowers some grieving loved ones leave on graves as "inappropriate and tacky."

A public cemetery in an English town banned plastic flowers and ornaments on graves, only to have to repeal the ban when there was an outcry from loved ones. A cemetery in another part of the country instituted a similar ban because the plastic flowers were continually getting caught in the lawnmowers and the bits of flying plastic constituted a health hazard.

Roadside memorials for people who died in traffic accidents are prohibited in Pell City, Alabama.

Some teens, extremely desperate for some fun (or at least something to talk about) have discovered embalming fluid as a new drug. Authorities caught on to the trend when more and more funeral homes started to report theft of the substance. A cigarette is dipped in the substance then smoked, producing a hallucinogenic effect. It's illegal according to US federal drug law.

*The mourning widow realized too late that she should
have sprung for the corrugated coffin.*

Thinking Outside the Box

Is it illegal to be buried in a cardboard casket in Australia?
Funeral directors say "yes," while an environmentally friendly casket company—whose biodegradable product is made

from 100% recycled cardboard caskets—says "no." The catch is in the phrasing of statutes in certain states. The law says that caskets must be made of timber or "another substantial material" or a product "derived from timber," which would include cardboard.

Stayin' Alive

With his local cemetery filling up and federal restrictions on expansion of the existing space or construction of a new one, as well as a prohibition on cremation due to environmental factors, the mayor of Biritba Mirim, Brazil decided to pass a ban on dying. While there is no penalty for the offense, the statute makes clear that individuals are expected to take care of themselves to try to prevent the inevitable. The cemetery—which has served the community since 1910—reached capacity some time ago and the town has been forced to send its former citizens into the afterlife in shared accommodations.

Is it really illegal to die in the British Houses of Parliament? Not exactly. The law, which dates back hundreds of years, states that anyone who dies in a royal palace (which includes Parliament) is entitled to a state funeral, which is an expense that the government tries to avoid.

Dead Men Don't Play Online Games

A Japanese woman was arrested for virtually killing her online husband—sort of. The charges against the woman were for illegal computer access after she hacked the account of a man who played her husband in an online game, and then "virtually" murdered him. The woman, a player on Maple Story (an online game in which players create a virtual identity and then establish social relationships), was angry that her online husband had divorced her. She took login information that she had gotten from the real life person who played her online husband and used it to log in to the game and then kill him. The man contacted police when he tried

Hell hath no fury like a virtual woman scorned.

to play the game and found out that he couldn't because he was dead. Police said that there was no indication that the woman had real-life plans to kill the actual person who had played her online husband.

There Are No Traffic Tickets in Heaven

The traffic cops on the beat in Gainesville, Florida are no slackers. When a white BMW parked illegally on a city street was not removed, they continued to issue citations (seven in all) for two weeks. It was only after that time that they discovered that the driver was actually in the car, slumped over into the backseat, dead.

Dying to Be with Jane and Walt . . . and Fido

The long-dead British author Jane Austen has legions of devoted fans all over the world. So devoted are they that their dying wish is to be with Jane for eternity. The Jane Austen Museum—a 17th century cottage in Hampshire where the

It's not going to be easy collecting on these tickets.

author once lived—had to outlaw people scattering loved ones' ashes around the property because the many mounds that began to appear were "distressing for the gardener and of no horticultural value to the garden."

Although Walt Disney World officials deny it, others, including former employees, report that there have been numerous cases of scattered ashes at the theme park, particularly at the Haunted Mansion, but also the Pirates of the Caribbean ride.

A Washington state legislator proposed a bill that would allow humans and their beloved pets to be buried together. The law, which only covers cats and dogs, would override legislation that states that cemeteries are for human remains only.

Closing Arguments

WELL, ladies and gentlemen of the jury, you've seen the evidence. Now it's up to you. Are these laws in the best interest of public health and safety? Or are they just there to ensure that we safely continue to have a healthy public debate? Do these laws help maintain order or just order us to maintain some pretty weird standards?

Whatever you decide, rest assured that this is not the end of the discussion. For every crazy, archaic law that is stricken from the books, a new possibly even crazier one will take its place. And don't forget, there are many new vast frontiers of law yet to be explored. Lawmakers in the European Union, Australia, the UK, and fifteen US states have already started to pass legislation on human reproductive cloning, but that doesn't mean that that hamburger you're eating for dinner isn't from cloned beef (that's legal in most places, although it has to be labeled). Cyber spying laws are just starting to be developed. The US even graduated its first space lawyer (that is a lawyer with a certificate in space law) in 2008. But as we approach many new legal horizons, there will still be many who look to the past instead of the future: A new anti-blasphemy law was passed in Ireland in 2009 (even as the UK moved to repeal one from the Middle Ages). And laws that once seemed pretty silly (that one about spitting on sidewalks) sometimes start to make sense again (the law was reconsidered after the swine flu outbreak in 2008 since the disease can be transferred through saliva).

You will have to be the ones who decides the important issues of the future: Should people be allowed to divorce via text message? Should Hummers should be banned from public roads? Take your time. Give these items your full consideration. But don't stress too much. There's always room for an appeal.

Index

INDEX

INDEX

INDEX